Knowing the Author of Your Faith

A Study of Hebrews

Wes and Elaine Willis

ACCENT PUBLICATIONS
Colorado Springs, Colorado

Accent Publications
P.O. Box 36640
4050 Lee Vance View
Colorado Springs, Colorado   80936

Copyright © 1996 Accent Publications
Printed in the United States of America

Library of Congress Catalog Card Number 95-79336

ISBN 0-89636-321-X

CONTENTS

Introduction to Hebrews

The New Testament book of Hebrews is a truly rich source of spiritual insight about our Lord and Savior Jesus Christ. More than any other New Testament book, it teaches us about the ministry of Christ, especially His continuing ministry after God raised Him from the dead.

We don't know for sure who the original recipients of this letter were, but the text does give us some clues. We can be sure that these people were well-versed in the Old Testament Scriptures.

In the introduction to Hebrews in *The Ryrie Study Bible,* Dr. Ryrie writes that the author quotes the Old Testament 29 times and refers to 53 other Old Testament passages. This would suggest that Hebrews was directed to a group of Jewish Christians who were growing in their understanding of the Gospel.

Several key themes reappear throughout the book. The word "better" is used repeatedly to explain the relationship between the Old Testament system and Christianity. And it soon becomes apparent to the reader that Jesus is a key theme. In fact these two themes are bound together throughout the book. Jesus is better—better than the angels, better than Moses, better than the Old Testament high priests, and a better sacrifice. "Heavenly" and "perfection" are also themes that we encounter regularly.

One of the issues that scholars have debated for years is the question of who wrote the book of Hebrews. Traditionally, Paul has been suggested as the author. Certainly his extensive knowledge of the Old Testament (Philippians 3:5) coupled with his deep devotion to Christ would support this position as would the mention of his bonds (10:34), Italy (13:24), and Timothy (13:23). But the fact that he is not identified as the author (as in all of his other epistles) raises some question. When translating Hebrews from the Greek, it becomes obvious that both the vocabulary and the literary style differ from Paul's. This has led scholars to suggest other authors.

Other candidates for having written Hebrews include one of Paul's early companions, Barnabas. A number of those from the first few centuries suggested Barnabas, and some even referred to Hebrews as The Epistle of Barnabas. Another of the early church fathers (Clement of Alexandria) suggested that Paul wrote the original manuscript in Hebrew (Paul's native language) and that Luke translated it into Greek. Other speculations include Apollos, Silas, and Priscilla and Aquila.

Whoever wrote Hebrews and whoever were the original recipients, we can be sure of two things. First, we can be sure that it was written under the guidance of the Holy Spirit. There is no question that it is inspired Scripture, given to us by God. Hebrews is accurate, reliable, and profitable for our study and spiritual growth.

Second, we can be sure that its truths apply to us today. Each of us needs to come to a deeper appreciation of the profound ministry of Jesus Christ. It is our prayer that as you study this book, you will come to know and love Christ more fully. May God's Spirit guide you in your understanding and application of the book of Hebrews as you study its truths in the coming weeks.

1

"SHE SAID DEFINE SUPERIOR, AND I PUT JESUS. WHAT'S WRONG WITH THAT?"

Jesus — Better Than the Angels
HEBREWS 1:1-14

*I*t is unfortunate that we often fail to give respect to those who deserve it. In some societies, the elder members of the community are accorded that high level of respect. Young people are taught to defer to their elders, and the needs and opinions of older adults are elevated above the needs and opinions of those who are younger.

Once, while visiting a friend's house with several college students, the host was taking us on a tour of his very interesting house. One student (a young lady) had come from Burma to study in the United States. As we approached the stairway, Wes stepped aside to allow the woman student to go up the stairs first. She looked somewhat uncomfortable and insisted, "Oh no, you go first."

In spite of her deference, Wes encouraged her to go ahead. She replied that she would rather not, and that she was struggling to adjust to our custom of men stepping aside and allowing women to go first. She explained that she had been taught that younger people always allowed those who were older to precede them. In her country, respect related more to age than to gender.

As we begin the book of Hebrews, we encounter one of its key themes in the very first chapter. It relates to respect and priority. God wants us to understand that Jesus has priority over all created beings. The first category of created beings to which God compares Jesus is angels. In the first century, when this epistle was written, angels were revered highly. But Jesus deserves a value and respect far above angels. This is not to say that angels are unimportant, but Jesus is in a totally different category. The angels are created beings, created to worship and to serve. But Jesus is the Son of God, the One whom we (and angels) worship and serve.

HOW GOD COMMUNICATED
(Hebrews 1:1-3)

One critically important truth about God is that He has spoken to us. He chose to communicate in a variety of ways over the centuries. And in the completed, written Scriptures, we can know what God communicated to humanity.

1. (1:1) *God spoke to the prophets in various (divers) ways. What were some of the ways God chose to communicate His truth to the prophets?*

❏ *Why was it important for God to communicate to mankind?*

❏ What importance does the scriptural record of the Old Testament prophets have in your life?

2. (1:2) The *"last days"* refer to the historical setting when the book of Hebrews was written. In what way(s) did God speak to us through His Son Jesus?

❏ How does the fact that Jesus is the heir of all created things and also the Creator lend authority to what He said?

❏ Since we are part of what Jesus created, how ought we to respond to Him?

3. (1:3) List the three significant characteristics of Jesus identified here.

 •

 •

 •

❏ Why are these qualifications important to Jesus' ability to pay for our sins?

❏ What is the significance of the statement that Jesus *"had by himself purged our sins"*?

❐ *What is the significance of the statement that, after paying for our sin, Jesus sat down?*

❐ *Do we still need prophets today or is the revealed Word made flesh enough?*

THE ROLE OF THE ANGELS
(Hebrews 1:4-7)

As important as the angels are, they pale in the light of Jesus, the Son of God. Part of the superiority of Jesus grows out of His relationship to His Father.

1. (1:4) *What name did Jesus inherit from His Father?*

2. (1:5) *The fact that Jesus was begotten of God does not mean that Jesus began at some specific time. Rather, He shares the very essence of God, including having no beginning or ending. How is this different from the angels?*

❐ *What relationship does God have with the angels?*

3. (1:6) *What does it mean that God brought the first begotten into the world?*

❐ *Why is it appropriate for angels to worship Jesus?*

❏ *If angels, who have a level of power and glory above ours, worship Jesus, how much more should we? What are some of the ways in which you worship Jesus?*

❏ *What are some other elements or activities that would honor Jesus and which you could include in your worship?*

JESUS NEVER CHANGES
(Hebrews 1:7-12)

We all know about things wearing out. Our clothing, for instance, becomes worn and threadbare, and we throw it out. But Jesus never changes. Just as He was, He is, and He shall always be. Even creation changes, but Jesus never does.

1. (1:7-8) *The form of angels changes depending on their assignment. They may appear as wind (spirits) or fire, but always their function is serving as ministers. How is Jesus different from this?*

2. (1:9) *Verse 9 describes how Jesus lived when He was on the earth. What characterized Jesus' behavior?*

❏ *How did God anoint Jesus with the "oil of gladness above thy fellows"?*

11

❐ *What implications does verse 9 have for the way in which you ought to live as a follower of Jesus?*

3. (1:10) *What are some characteristics of our world that point to the Creator?*

❐ *Since Jesus made us (as part of the created world), and then gave His life in payment for our sin, He desires a response from us. Have you personally accepted Jesus' payment for your sin? If not, will you pause right now and pray? Tell God that you know that you are a sinner and that you believe Jesus died to pay for your sin and rose from the grave to give you life everlasting. Thank God that on the basis of faith alone, He makes you one of His children and gives you eternal life.*

4. (1:11-12) *God views creation as we view worn-out clothing. In contrast, Jesus is eternal and changeless. How does the way in which we dispose of worn out clothing give us insight to God's views of His creation?*

❐ *How do some people show they value clothing or other material things more than those things which are eternal?*

❐ *In contrast to the temporary nature of garments, what are some other Scriptures that elaborate on or describe the nature of Jesus?*

❏ How do we as Christians demonstrate our dependence on Jesus as eternal and changeless?

THE DUTIES OF ANGELS
(Hebrews 1:13-14)

A significant distinction between Jesus and the angels is that Jesus reigns while the angels have been given the responsibility of serving.

1. (1:13) What two major features distinguish the role of Jesus Christ from that of the angels?

❏ What does this tell you about Jesus' authority?

❏ What are some ways you can consciously acknowledge His authority over your life as you interact with people who come under your responsibility or authority?

2. (1:14) What are some of the ways recorded in the Bible that angels ministered to God's children?

❏ What are some ways in which angels might minister to us today?

DIGGING DEEPER

1. Read Acts 12:1-19. Apparently God chose to preserve Peter's life, but not James's. We don't know why this was, but we can be sure that it was appropriate in God's infinite wisdom. How did God use His angel in this account? How did this angel minister to Peter?

❏ Peter apparently did not know immediately that it was an angel that came to him. How might you or others have been helped by an angel without recognizing it as such?

❏ What insight does Matthew 18:10 add to this concept?

2. Since angels were created to serve, and Jesus Himself served His followers (John 13:12-17), what example does this give to us?

❏ In what ways are you serving Jesus by serving others?

Fellow Christians   **_Non-Christians_**

3. *This created world is of temporary duration (Hebrews 1:10-12; II Peter 3:10-13). But how would you describe the attitude of most people living in North America toward the material world?*

❒ *In what ways do Christians become ensnared by this viewpoint?*

❒ *If we truly looked at life from God's perspective, how would it change our attitudes toward the following areas of life?*

Our Jobs —

Our Homes —

Our Hobbies —

Our Material Possessions —

Our Relationships —

❖

2

Jesus — Our Suffering Sacrifice
HEBREWS 2:1-18

At various times all of us need assistance from those who know more than we do. Perhaps we are drafting a will, setting up a retirement plan, or buying a house, and we need the knowledge and counsel of an expert in that particular field.

At one point in the growth of our family we observed that our sons were becoming more and more interested in downhill skiing. We felt that their interest in skiing would increase and that we could enjoy this activity together as a family. But as their parents, we faced a dilemma—we didn't know how to ski. After the first or second outing, with the boys skiing and us waiting for them in the lodge, we knew that we faced a decision. Unless we also learned to ski, these trips were going to become very long and extremely boring. So we decided to get some skiing instruction.

But we wanted to take ski lessons from someone who knew how to ski and who also knew how to teach skiing. For us, this was made quite simple because the ski resort offered instruction packages using only fully-certified instructors. And so we made the leap. Each of us took lessons and began skiing. Apparently the instructors were competent because both of us have learned how to ski, have avoided injury (sore muscles excluded), and we have shared many enjoyable experiences as a family.

When we search out an expert in spiritual matters, we find that Jesus' qualifications are impeccable. He can meet our needs. As both God and Man, He alone was able to bridge the gap between us and God—the gap caused by our sin. And the author of Hebrews emphasizes the fact that it is important that we listen carefully to Jesus both because of *who He is* and also because of *what He has done.*

WARNING AGAINST DRIFTING
(Hebrews 2:1-4)

*T*his is the first of the five warning passages in Hebrews. In this warning, we are challenged not to be careless in our obedience to the Word; we must not drift away from our commitment.

1. **(2:1)** *Many have heard the truth of God's Word for years. What are some of the ways in which we might "let slip" (literally, drift away from) those things that we have heard?*

❒ *Even a mature Christian who has studied and applied spiritual truth over the years can become careless about obedience. Suggest some things that you can do to prevent carelessness about following God's Word.*

2. (2:2) *Angels participated in the giving of the Old Covenant (cf. Galatians 3:19) and people were careful to pay attention. The word translated angel literally means messenger. Who were some of the messengers through whom God chose to communicate the Old Testament Scriptures?*

❏ *What was the outcome of their messages?*

3. (2:3-4) *Why is the fact that the New Testament message came directly from Christ and not from a messenger significant?*

❏ *How should this influence how we look at obedience?*

❏ *What were some of the ways that God confirmed the reliability of the message from Jesus?*

❏ *What are some ways that God has confirmed the reliability of His Word to you personally?*

THE EXCELLENCE OF JESUS
(Hebrews 2:5-9)

*E*ven though angels (and other messengers) played a significant role in the revelation from God, they have not been given the position and the authority that Jesus has. And He received this authority because God granted it to Him.

1. (2:5) *In what ways does Jesus have the authority over the world order that is coming?*

❏ *What are some of the areas in your life where Jesus has authority right now?*

❏ *Identify one or more areas where you have been reluctant to allow Him to rule.*

2. (2:6-7) *This is a quotation of Psalm 8:4-6. What are some ways in which human beings are lower than angels?*

❏ *And how are human beings placed in a position of honor before God?*

❏ *Since we have been set over the works of God's hands, we have a responsibility as stewards of God's creation. How should this influence the way that we treat...*

-The environment

-Other people

-Our own bodies

❑ Who are some people that you should be treating differently because of your stewardship responsibility? What should you be doing differently?

Person   **_Do Differently_**

3. (2:8) What are some things that are in subjection to Jesus now?

❑ What has yet to be put under Him?

4. (2:9) What does it mean that Jesus was made "a little lower than the angels" (cf. 2:7)?

❑ What did God do for Jesus because of the position that He accepted?

❑ How does Jesus' attitude provide a good example for us?

❑ What are some areas where you may have been demanding your rights rather than giving them up so that you can serve others as Jesus did?

THE WORK OF JESUS
(Hebrews 2:10-18)

*T*o think that Jesus Christ became a human being and suffered as He did is astounding. But it is because of what Jesus did for us that we can become God's children and can know the blessing of having Jesus Christ for our brother.

1. (2:10-11) *Jesus, the Captain of our salvation was made perfect (literally, complete) through His suffering. How and why did it require suffering for Jesus to be completed in His work?*

❑ *How does it make you feel when you realize that it was for you that Jesus suffered?*

❑ *How have you responded to what He has done?*

❑ *Who is the sanctifier and who are the sanctified; how have the two been brought together?*

❑ *In what ways does the fact that you have been sanctified by the work of Jesus influence how you live each day?*

2. (2:12-13) *Ordinarily we think of Christians singing praises to Jesus. But here Jesus sings our praises. Why would He do that?*

❏ Why might Jesus have described us both as His brothers and also as His children within just a few verses?

3. (2:14-16)   How were humans held in bondage to death?

❏ How has that been changed because of what Jesus did?

❏ What difference does it make at the funeral of a Christian loved one to know that we are not in bondage to death?

❏ What difference does it make in your praying and worshiping when you remember that Jesus became flesh and blood, a human being, just as you are?

4. (2:17)   What are some of the ways in which Jesus was made like human beings?

❏ What difference did it make that He also kept His divine nature—He continued to be God?

5. (2:18)   To "succour" someone means to comfort or encourage. Because Jesus suffered great pain and temptation, we can know that Jesus truly is sensitive to how we feel. What

are some areas/problems today in which you particularly need the comfort that only can come from Jesus?

❏ Take a few moments to pray about these areas; ask Jesus to provide the comfort only He can give.

DIGGING DEEPER

1. One of the contemporary "causes" that some have espoused is an animal rights agenda. Those who take this position seem to elevate animals to the level of humans, and they stress that we have no right to use animals for food or to serve humans. How do the truths contained in this passage help us to have a more accurate understanding of the relationship between humans and animals?

❏ What are some of the ways in which the gap between humans and animals is far greater than the gap between angels and humans?

❏ What is the difference between using and abusing animals?

❏ What are some potential outcomes of viewing animals and humans as sharing all rights in common?

2. *Those who have accepted Christ as Saviour have been placed under the authority of Christ. How does this influence your actions and decisions in the following areas?*

— *Choice of Vocation (work)*

— *Relationships with family*

— *How you spend your money*

— *What you do in your spare time*

❑ *In which of these areas of your life would you like to see changes?*

❑ *What changes would be appropriate to make in these areas of your life?*

3. *One of the great ministries of Jesus is that He comforts and encourages us. And He is able to do that because of what He suffered. According to Paul's teaching (II Corinthians 1:3-4), we also can have the same kind of ministry. List some things in your life that have been unpleasant experiences, or some times when you have suffered.*

❒ *How could these life experiences have made you ready to help and to be more sensitive to the needs of others, perhaps those who may experience similar difficulties?*

❒ *Identify one person who needs to be encouraged—a person with whom you can share. What ways can you comfort or encourage that person?*

3

"HOW COME THEY SENT YOU TO OBEDIENCE SCHOOL AND EXPECT ME TO DO IT ON MY OWN?"

The Danger of Unbelief
HEBREWS 3:1-19

*N*ow that our sons are in their twenties, it is interesting to hear them talk about things they did when they were much younger. Not long ago, one of our sons filled in some details about the time he flew over the handlebars of his bike when he was a pre-schooler. When he landed, he knocked out one tooth and cut his face, especially his upper lip, very badly. The worst part was that we were tent camping at a state park, and when it happened, Wes was away with the car. So we had to wait to get treatment until hours after the accident. What we, the parents, discovered just recently was that our son who had the accident was trying to ride his older brother's bike—a full-sized bicycle—and he was only four!

Perhaps it's just as well we didn't know all the details at the time. Because if we had, we probably would have used one of those phrases that all children dread hearing. "Maybe this will be a lesson to you." At some time during child rearing, most parents will echo that phrase, and all children hate to hear it.

But the fact is that we *should* learn from our own experience. And if we really are wise, we also will learn from the experiences of others. The author of Hebrews suggests that Israel's experiences should serve as lessons to us. When Israel was about to enter the Promised Land, they drew back from fear and intimidation. Of the twelve spies that Moses sent to reconnoiter in the Promised Land, only two encouraged Israel to occupy the land. In direct disobedience to God, Israel followed the advice of the ten. They rebelled against God and refused to enter the land. Because of their rebellion, Israel wandered in the wilderness for 40 years. And all except Joshua and Caleb perished in the wilderness during those 40 years.

The author of Hebrews warns us to learn from their example. We must not draw back in disobedience. If we do, like Israel, we may well forfeit the blessings that God wants to give to us.

JESUS COMPARED TO MOSES
(Hebrews 3:1-6)

*G*od's Word came to us through both Moses and Jesus Christ. But even though both faithfully communicated God's Word, they had dramatically different roles. Because of who Jesus is, we should be particularly careful about obeying His instruction.

1. (3:1) *Notice the two descriptions of Jesus. He is called an Apostle (one who represents God to man), and a High Priest (one who represents man to God). List below some of Jesus' ministries to you through these relationships.*

• Apostle —   *• High Priest —*

2. (3:2-6) *These verses compare Moses' and Jesus' ministries and picture them as seen in relation to a household. In the chart below fill in the comparisons between Moses and Jesus.*

	MOSES	JESUS
Faithfulness (verse 2)		
Glory (verse 3)		
Roles . (verses 5-6)		

❒ *The Jews took the Law of Moses very seriously. Since Jesus is so much more important than Moses, why do you think Christians today are often careless about obeying Christ's teachings?*

WARNING AGAINST DISOBEDIENCE (Hebrews 3:7-11)

*T*his section begins the second major warning in Hebrews. The warning actually extends through Hebrews 4:11, but we will study it in several sections for convenience. Verses 7-11 (a direct quotation of Psalm 95:7-11) comprise an explanation of the background to the warning—Israel's disobedience at Kadesh-Barnea when they refused to enter the Promised Land.

1. (3:7-9) *"Wherefore" indicates that this portion builds on the preceding verses and is a logical outcome of those verses. Since the exhortation is a specific command to obedience, how do verses 1-6 naturally lead into this?*

❒ *The refusal to enter the Promised Land at Kadesh-Barnea was the final act, but there were other instances of disobedience. The "provocation" and the "temptation" may refer to Exodus 17:1-7 (complaining about no water just after leaving Egypt) and Numbers 20:1-3 (again complaining about no water). What was God's final judgment for Israel's repeated disobedience?*

❒ *What does the fact that God gave Israel many chances tell you about His nature?*

❒ *In what situations might you be prone to complain about what you think God might not be doing for you?*

❒ *How does Israel's experience both comfort and warn you?*

2. (3:10-11) *Even though entering the Promised Land required work and many battles, God described it as rest. Rest is not "doing nothing"; rather, it is enjoying God's blessing as we obey Him. How is God's blessing to us tied directly to work?*

❒ *How might your heart attitude keep you from experiencing God's blessing?*

❏ What are some of "God's ways" (verse 10) that Christians today might not know or follow?

❏ How would we expect this to impact our enjoyment of God's rest (blessings)?

GOD'S CHALLENGE TO US
(Hebrews 3:12-15)

*E*ven God's children are tempted to sin and disobey Him. It is important to recognize that such sin carries consequences. And although He will not dismiss us from His family, we certainly will not enjoy the blessings that Christ has promised to us.

1. (3:12) How do we know that the author is addressing Christians in this verse?

❏ How is disobedience "departing from the living God?"

❏ Why is unbelief part of it?

2. (3:13) What is the antidote for the disease of unbelief?

❏ How is sin "deceitful" and why does it harden Christians?

❏ *What are some reasons that Christians might be hesitant to exhort other believers who may have sin-hardened hearts?*

❏ *How might God hold us responsible if we know a fellow Christian who is disobeying God and we refuse to confront that brother or sister?*

3. (3:14-15) *"Partakers of Christ" does not refer to whether or not we are saved. It deals with fellowship with Christ in this life and enjoying the blessings of obedience. What is necessary to enjoy the blessings of Christ?*

❏ *How might a person begin one way and end another?*

❏ *How might you hear the "voice of God" today?*

❏ *List some Christians in your current circle of acquaintances who might need exhortation from you to continue in faith and obedience. How could you help them?*

A REMINDER OF ISRAEL'S DISOBEDIENCE
(Hebrews 3:16-19)

What happened to Israel is a warning to us today. Those who hardened their hearts suffered the consequences of their disobedience—they missed the blessings of the Promised Land that God wanted to give them.

1. (3:16) *God allows us the freedom to choose obedience or disobedience, but He clearly warns us of the consequences. Why do you think that almost all of the Israelites who came out of Egypt chose not to believe that God could give them victory in the Promised Land?*

❏ *What might be some key elements that influence whether believers today obey God or harden their hearts?*

❏ *How do you make sure that your heart remains pliable and sensitive to God?*

❏ *What do you do if you feel a spiritual coldness setting in or if you feel tempted to disobey God's Word?*

2. (3:17) *Some people view God as a kindly, non-condemning, old man. Others view Him as a vengeful judge, delighting in punishing those who "step out of line." How does this verse contradict both of those heresies?*

❏ *How can the true nature of God cause us both to fear and also to be comforted?*

3. (3:18-19) *Even though God warned Israel of the consequences, they still disobeyed. What people today seem to respond just like the Israelites?*

❏ What warning would you give to such a person?

❏ What are some scriptural truths that may sometimes be difficult for you to believe and act on?

❏ How could a believer strengthen his or her resolve to believe God and follow such biblical truths?

DIGGING DEEPER

1. Read Numbers 13:17—14:10. What assignment did Moses give to the spies (13:18-20)?

❏ How does Numbers 13:2 indicate that it really didn't matter what the spies found in the land if Israel had believed God?

❏ Contrast the attitude of the ten who gave a negative report with Joshua and Caleb.

Attitude of the Ten   **Attitude of the Two**

❏ What personal applications can you make about obedience to God and trusting Him for the outcomes?

2. Almost all of the Jews who came out of Egypt died in the wilderness because of their rebellion and sin. They did not receive the Promised Land blessings. Think about the New Testament church today. Do you see any parallels of not receiving blessings for similar reasons?

❏ We have the written Word of God and also the example of Jesus who is the living Word of God. List some of the actions and attitudes demonstrated by Jesus when He was on the earth that are examples we should follow if we want to enjoy the blessing of God.

❏ How might some who are disobedient influence the church to go along with their sinful attitudes or actions and thus cause the entire church to miss out on God's blessing?

❏ This week pray specifically for discernment and godliness for your local church's lay and pastoral leadership, as well as for biblical harmony among all church members.

❖

4

"I USUALLY CALL JESUS."

Jesus — Our Faithful Helper
HEBREWS 4:1—5:10

Several years ago Wes and our three sons, along with some adventuresome friends, took a short backpacking trip in the Ozark Mountains. It was early spring and the weather was cool, but beautiful. The Ozark mountains in northern Arkansas are not as rugged as some other mountain ranges in the United States. Nevertheless, there is no level ground. Virtually all of the hiking is uphill or down.

In our hiking group, there were several other adults and a couple of younger boys who had not done much backpacking. We anticipated having to help some of the younger members due to their inexperience, and we made sure that their packs were not too heavy. We purposely had them carry much of the food that we would be eating, to ensure that their packs would become progressively lighter after each meal.

Surprisingly, the younger boys presented no problems. But we faced a serious difficulty with one of the most experienced campers in the group who, unknowingly, had contracted a flu-like infection just before leaving home. This didn't affect him very much at first, but with each day he grew significantly weaker. Soon it became obvious that our friend was struggling desperately to keep up. More and more frequently we had to stop for him to rest.

At every break, each of us would remove something from our friend's pack and put it into our own. By the third day, our friend had nothing left in his pack. We had distributed all of his gear throughout our packs. We were carrying his load; but no one complained, because we knew how he felt and how much he needed the help. We all had experienced the weakness that comes with illness. And we felt his pain deeply.

The author of Hebrews reminds us that Jesus, our high priest, is sensitive to our needs. He knows what we are going through because he also suffered. Because he understands and is compassionate, we can come to Him for help at any time. He's waiting to carry our loads—if only we'll let Him.

THE WARNING AGAINST UNBELIEF RESTATED (Hebrews 4:1-10)

*T*his restatement of the second warning serves as a reminder: It is possible that after we hear the Word of God and begin a Christian walk of obedience, we may later choose to disobey and ultimately miss out on the blessings God wants to give us.

1. (4:1) *Name some of the blessings that God has promised to you (and to all Christians).*

❏ *Under what circumstances might it be possible that we would forfeit those blessings due to disobedience?*

2. (4:2-3) *How do Christians today fit into two categories similar to God's chosen people, the Israelites (those who trusted God's promise and wanted to enter the Promised Land and those who did not)?*

❏ *What makes the difference between the two categories?*

❏ *Which category would you put yourself in and what examples from your life illustrate that conclusion?*

❏ *How does it make you feel to know that God's rest (blessings) was not an afterthought but was planned at creation for you?*

3. (4:4-5) *How does God's rest on the seventh day after creation provide an example to us in our work?*

❏ *Why do you think some Christians today are uptight and feel stressed out?*

❏ *What would you suggest as a help to those who might feel that way?*

❒ What are some ways you seek to keep balance between ministry and rest in your Christian walk?

4. (4:6-7) The generation of Israelites whom God wanted to take into the Promised Land refused to believe in His power, so God waited to give the fulfillment of His promise to the next generation. What are some blessings that God might want to give the church today that we refuse to accept?

❒ What conditions do you think would need to exist for God to bestow those blessings on His church?

5. (4:8-10) The name "Jesus" (Jehovah saves) is the Greek translation of the Hebrew name "Joshua." In the context here, it is apparent that the author is referring to the Israelite leader, Joshua, who could not give the Jews ultimate rest. What was the earthly rest (blessing) that God wanted to give His people in Joshua's day?

❒ What is the eternal rest (blessing) that Joshua could not give?

❒ How is the fact that God rested a proof of the fact that we can look forward with certainty to eternal rest?

RECEIVING THE BLESSINGS OF GOD
(Hebrews 4:11-13)

We need to give great attention to our belief, but we are not left to our own devices in this spiritual endeavor. Rather, God has given us a great resource to strengthen our faith.

1. (4:11) *At first glance, it seems that we are being told to work very hard at resting. But actually the text encourages us to see the importance of accepting the rest of God. How is the simple belief that you demonstrated when you accepted Christ a good illustration of what your continuing attitude should be?*

❏ *What might get in the way of continued simple belief?*

2. (4:12) *Both the written Word (the Bible) and the Living Word (Jesus) help us to understand God's will and how we should live. What are the three pairs that the Word of God distinguishes between (divides asunder)?*

❏ *Is it humanly possible for us to distinguish between the elements in each pair?*

❏ *What descriptions of the Word of God (perhaps of both Jesus and the Bible) does the author of Hebrews give?*

❏ *How does the Word of God help you understand the motivation for the things that you do?*

❏ How could you become more sensitive to this role of the Word in your life?

3. (4:13) How does it make you feel to know that God knows and understands everything about you, even your motivations?

❏ How does it serve as an encouragement and as a deterrent?

❏ What difference should it make in how you demonstrate God's love to difficult people around you if you remember that God knows everything about you and still loves you totally?

JESUS OUR COMPASSIONATE HIGH PRIEST (Hebrews 4:14-5:10)

*T*o many Christians, one of the most meaningful truths about Jesus is that He understands what we are going through. Jesus experienced all of the kinds of difficulties that we face in life, and He represents us before God.

1. (4:14) How does the fact that Jesus is in Heaven demonstrate His ability to intercede for us before God and that His sacrifice has been accepted by God?

❏ "Hold fast" means to cling to or act on the basis of our profession (what we have said that we believe). How does the work of Jesus encourage us to act on what we believe?

2. (4:15) *A high priest represented man before God. On what basis can we feel confident that Jesus understands what we feel and struggle with?*

❒ *Why is it important to you that Jesus understands how you feel?*

❒ *List three or four ways Jesus suffered when He was here on earth and how those events relate to struggles you have had in your life.*

3. (4:16) *What attitude should we have when we approach Jesus' throne?*

❒ *Mercy means not giving us what we deserve, and grace is giving us what we don't deserve. How would you illustrate the mercy and grace that Jesus grants us when we ask?*

4. (5:1-3) *What were the primary functions of a high priest?*

❒ *Why was it important for the worshiper to know that the high priest understood and was sensitive to the worshiper's needs?*

5. (5:4-6) *What significance do you see in the fact that God had two orders of priests (Aaron and Melchisedec)?*

❏ *Look at Genesis 14:18 and Zechariah 6:12-13. How is Jesus different from the Aaronic priests?*

6. (5:7-10) *When in Jesus' life did He go through the experiences mentioned in verse 7?*

❏ *How do the experiences described in verses 7 and 8 encourage you to come to Jesus for help?*

❏ *Are there any situations you are currently trying to handle on your own, instead of sharing them with Jesus? What are some specific steps you can take to appropriate His help?*

❏ *In verse 9 the word "perfect" means to be made complete or fully mature. How did Jesus' experiences on earth complete His preparation to be our faithful high priest?*

DIGGING DEEPER

1. *Read Philippians 4:6-7. Paul seems to suggest that some people would rather worry than pray. How does the exhortation in Hebrews 4:15-16 provide an alternative to anxiety?*

❏ What are some things that you tend to worry about?

❏ How does the grace of God enable us to deal with worry appropriately?

2. Since we have been admonished to come to God's throne to receive mercy and grace, we should do it regularly. This means both systematic (following a prayer list) and spontaneous (as needs arise) praying. When do you schedule regular time to pray and meet God before His throne?

❏ When do you pray spontaneously?

❏ How do you make sure that your prayer life is not haphazard?

❏ What changes do you need to make in your prayer habits to enable you to be more regular and systematic in your praying?

❖

5

"I WONDER WHAT FRUIT THEY'RE PRODUCING."

Growing Up Spiritually
HEBREWS 5:11—6:20

*M*ost of us can remember unusual things that we thought or did when we were children. We look back on some of those beliefs or actions and marvel that we ever behaved in such a way.

We knew one child who insisted that he had to eat the foods on his dinner plate one at a time. He would select an item of food and finish eating all of that one food. Then he would move on to the next item. He ate all of his meals this way, one food at a time. Another child was horrified if any one type of food touched another. He insisted on separation of his foods, even to not allowing his spaghetti sauce to touch the pasta!

Many children imagine or believe some pretty strange things. Some think that all dogs are males and all cats are females. Others insist that there are monsters in the closet or under the bed. Many of us had imaginary friends whom we insisted were real.

But at some point in life we need to move on to maturity. We come to understand basic principles of life and how things actually function. We establish values based on reality not imagination. And when this happens we can move into the role of helping and serving others. When we mature, we recognize our duty to help others. This portion of Hebrews addresses the issue of spiritual maturity and how we should act as "grown-ups."

CHARACTERISTICS OF SPIRITUAL IMMATURITY (Hebrews 5:11-14)

*T*he last four verses of chapter 5 and all of chapter 6 are a parenthesis in the flow of the argument of Hebrews. Instead of moving on to discuss Melchizedek, the author inserts a discussion of spiritual maturity. He begins by describing the Hebrew Christians in their present state.

1. (5:11) *Notice that "Of whom" refers back to Melchizedek in verse 10. Glance ahead to 7:1 and notice that the author picks up the same theme after this parenthesis. Why did the author not just continue teaching about Melchizedek?*

❐ *What do you think "dull of hearing" means?*

2. (5:12) *What ministry should the Hebrew Christians have been capable of doing?*

❐ *Instead, what need did they themselves have?*

❏ What are the "first principles" of the oracles of God?

❏ Which way would you describe yourself—a "milk" Christian or a "meat" Christian. Why?

3. (5:13-14) What physical comparison here describes a spiritual condition?

❏ How is this a particularly appropriate description?

❏ What doctrines or biblical truths would you classify as "milk" and as "meat"?

Milk   **Meat**

❏ What situations exist in your church today because of the Christians who do not have spiritual discernment?

❏ How could you contribute to improving the spiritual maturity in your church?

MOVING ON TOWARD MATURITY
(Hebrews 6:1-9)

*I*n order to understand these verses, it is important to remember the experience of Israel at Kadesh-Barnea.

They could either enter the Promised Land and receive the blessings (rest) promised by God, or they could choose not to go into the land. They made the wrong choice.

1. (6:1-3) *The Hebrew Christians were encouraged to move on toward maturity (perfection). But in order to do so, they had to stop feeding on milk alone. What are the "milk" doctrinal truths listed in these verses?*

❏ *Why do you think God wants us to move on from these elementary doctrines?*

2. (6:4-6) *What are some of the indicators that the people being addressed here actually were believers?*

❏ *Apparently some of the Hebrew believers who had not grown or had backslidden ("fall away") were trying to get "re-saved." If a person could be "re-saved," how would that "crucify to themselves the Son of God afresh?"*

❏ *Rather than getting "re-saved" what admonition from Hebrews 6:1 applied to these Christians?*

❏ *What do you need to do at this point in your Christian life to "go on unto perfection (maturity)?"*

3. (6:7-8) *What do the descriptions of the ground that produces good fruit (verse 7) and the ground that produces thorns (verse 8) illustrate?*

❏ *What is some of the good fruit that you observe fellow Christians producing?*

The thorns and briers (the worthless product of the ground) which are rejected indicate that God's judgment consumes any meaningless service. How is this an appropriate warning to Christians today?

4. (6:9) *What additional elements here demonstrate again that the author was addressing Christians?*

❏ *What are some of the things that should accompany salvation (that is, the normal things that should characterize Christians)?*

• *in personal lifestyle —*

• *in family relationships —*

• *in work/community relationships —*

• *in church relationships —*

THE DEPENDABILITY OF GOD'S PROMISES (Hebrews 6:10-20)

We know that God cannot lie (John 14:6; Titus 1:2). Therefore we can be sure that He will follow through on

His promises. But God also has confirmed His reliability by an oath.

1. (6:10) *How is this verse an encouragement to those who may be serving "behind the scenes," or those whose ministries are not publicly noticed?*

❐ *In what areas might you feel unrecognized or unappreciated?*

❐ *Why would it be unrighteous of God to forget your work and service done out of love for Him?*

❐ *What practical encouragement does this verse give you?*

2. (6:11-12) *What hope do these verses mean?*

❐ *Why are we encouraged to be diligent in ministering to the saints?*

❐ *What does verse 12 mean to you?*

3. (6:13-15) *In what ways does the fact that God made and fulfilled a humanly impossible promise to Abraham encourage you today?*

❒ How do you think Abraham felt as he grew old, waiting for God to fulfill His promise of an heir?

❒ What are some promises that it seems as though God has forgotten to fulfill for you?

4. (6:16-18) What are some things that people today swear by?

❒ Why do people take oaths and swear by something or someone greater than they are?

❒ The "two immutable things" in verse 18 refer back to verse 13. The first is that God gave His Word; the second, that He took an oath (or swore) that He would fulfill His promise. Why would God confirm to Abraham with two pledges, not just one?

❒ What does this tell you about the nature of God?

❒ How does this serve as a "strong consolation" to you?

5. (6:19-20) These verses introduce a new theme that resumes the topic of Melchizedek; the author reminds us that we can be confident and secure. What picture does the phrase "anchor of the soul" bring to your mind?

❐ *How will your confidence in the promises of God affect the way in which you approach life and service this week?*

DIGGING DEEPER

1. *The author of Hebrews compares spiritual immaturity to physical immaturity. Fill in column one below, listing characteristics of physical babies and adults. Then list some possible comparisons in the spiritual realm.*

Column 1	*Column 2*
Physical Babies	*Spiritual Babies*
Physical Adults	*Spiritual Adults*

❐ *Which group of spiritual characteristics above best describes you?*

❐ *Is this an encouragement or a discouragement, and why?*

❐ *What actions should you take based on this insight?*

❏ Match the doctrines of "milk" (Hebrews 6:1-2) with their descriptions.

___ The doctrine of Christ   a. Salvation through faith
___ Faith toward God   alone
___ Eternal judgment   b. The hope of the believer
___ Laying on of hands   c. Inability to save ourselves
___ Resurrection of the dead   d. Baptism as a symbol of
___ Baptism   faith in Christ
                                     e. Eternal punishment of the
                                     lost
                                     f. Basic truth about Christ's
                                     sacrifice

❏ Are you uncertain about any of these doctrines? Which ones? Be sure to ask your pastor or another mature leader to suggest resources for further study if you have questions.

2. Read I Corinthians 3:10-16 and compare it with Hebrews 6:8. How might the very same work of service at one time be "gold" and at another time be "stubble"? What makes the difference?

❏ List some areas of your service for God. What would you classify as "gold, silver, precious stones" types of service for God and what would be "wood, hay, stubble" service that God will reject?

❒ What might you do differently in the way you serve God as you consider this concept taught both in I Corinthians and Hebrews?

3. The promise of God to Abraham is recorded in Genesis 15 and 17. Not only did God promise that Abraham would become fruitful but also that he would become the father of a nation. Notice the promise in Genesis 15:4-6 and the covenant confirming the promise in Genesis 15:17-18. Why was it hard for Abraham to believe God's promise? (See Genesis 17:15-19.)

❒ What is the relationship between something being difficult for us to understand and God's ability to follow through on His promises?

❒ What are some of God's promises that are hard for you to believe? Why are they hard for you to believe?

❒ Confess any difficulty that you may have in believing God. Ask for His help to believe and to act on that belief.

❖

6

"THAT'S RIGHT, SON. THEY SACRIFICED WHOLE CALVES. EVEN THE HAMBURGER PART."

Jesus — Our High Priest
HEBREWS 7:1-28

*C*hildren often want to do tasks before they are able to do them. But then, when they finally are old enough, the excitement has gone.

Recently, we were watching a little girl pretend to vacuum the carpet. She had a toy vacuum cleaner and was working energetically at her imaginary task. But we can imagine what her attitude will be when she is old enough to use a functioning vacuum cleaner. Her parents may well find it takes more work to try to get her to vacuum the carpet than it would for them to do it themselves.

When our sons were young, they wanted desperately to be allowed to mow the grass. They would beg and plead, explaining how they knew what needed to be done and how they could be trusted to do it. But that was before they became mature enough to handle the lawn mower. When they were able to mow the lawn, the romance of the task quickly faded. They helped out when asked, and sometimes they even volunteered. But their enthusiasm was much less intense after they were old enough to do the job.

Even as there are certain tasks that require a substantial level of maturity, there are certain concepts, or ideas, that demand greater maturity. Chapter seven of Hebrews presents one of these concepts that requires spiritual understanding if the student is to grasp the truth. The author of Hebrews was ready to discuss this concept earlier. The end of chapter five and all of chapter six comprise a parenthesis in the flow of the argument of the book — to discuss the fact that many of the Hebrew Christians were not really mature enough to understand what he was about to teach.

Chapter seven presents Jesus as priest. Until the time of Christ, the priests were selected from those born of the tribe of Levi. But Jesus was of the tribe of Judah, not Levi. The author of Hebrews explains that Jesus' priesthood extends back long before Levi was born—back to the time of Abraham. Long before the Law was given and before the Levitical priesthood was established, Abraham paid tithes to Melchizedek. And Jesus is a priest, not in the line of Levi, but in the line of Melchizedek.

THE PERSON OF MELCHIZEDEK
(Hebrews 7:1-10)

*M*elchizedek is mentioned in two Old Testament passages—Genesis 14:17-20 (the historical event) and Psalm 110:4 (the prophetic passage about Jesus). Both of these passages help us better understand the verses in Hebrews 7.

1. (7:1-7) *Melchizedek clearly is a type, an Old Testament picture, of Christ. How do the interpretations of the name of Melchizedek describe Christ?*

❏ What does the fact that Abraham paid tithes to Melchizedek indicate about the way Abraham viewed him?

❏ What significance do you see in the action of Melchizedek blessing Abraham?

2. (7:3-4) *"Without father, without mother..." does not necessarily mean that Melchizedek had no parents or descendents, merely that we have no record of them. One of the two basic views is that Melchizedek was a man, but we have no record of his parents, so that he could be a picture of Christ. The other view is that Jesus actually appeared to Abraham as the priest Melchizedek. Whether a picture of Jesus or Jesus Himself, how is the description of Christ as a "priest continually"?*

❏ We learned why Moses was so important to the Jews (chapter 3). Why would Abraham have been even more important?

❏ Why is it significant that it was Abraham who paid tithes to Melchizedek?

❐ Why would Scripture point out that Abraham paid tithes before the giving of the Law? What importance would that have for believers today?

3. (7:5-7) *All Jews were descendants of Abraham. Those of the tribe of Levi were ordained by God to be the priests, and all other tribes paid tithes to them as God commanded because they did not receive an inheritance of land. Since Abraham paid tithes to Melchizedek and was blessed by him, what relationship do Abraham's descendants bear to Melchizedek?*

❐ What does it mean that "the less is blessed of the better" (verse 7)?

4. (7:8-10) *Why is it significant that we have no detailed record of Melchizedek's life or death?*

❐ Why would the author of Hebrews state that Abraham's descendants paid tithes to Melchizedek?

CONTRAST BETWEEN THE PRIESTHOODS (Hebrews 7:11-24)

*T*here are many great contrasts between the two priesthoods. It is important to recognize these differences. They are the basis of the wonderful work of Christ for us. Complete the chart below which contrasts the two priesthoods (Levi and Melchizedek) outlined in Hebrews 7.

	Levi	*Melchizedek*
Tribe	11,13	11,14
Qualifications	16	16-17
Standard	18	19
Results	19	19
Confirmation	21	20
Priests	23	22
Duration	23	24

❏ *How would worship be different if we still needed to approach God through Levitical priests today?*

❏ Do you think that the ease of approaching God today makes us more free or more careless about how we come to Him? Why?

❏ What can you do to become more serious about the way you approach God and to be more consistent in worshiping Him?

THE MINISTRY OF JESUS OUR HIGH PRIEST (Hebrews 7:25-28)

*T*he purpose of the Levitical priesthood was to represent the people to God. And Jesus, as our High Priest, fulfills the same function—perfectly.

1. (7:25) *Why is Jesus able to save us when the Levitical priests could not (cf. verse 19)?*

❏ What does it mean to you to know that Jesus intercedes with God for you?

2. (7:26) *How is Jesus is different from the Levitical priests?*

❏ Look at each quality descriptive of Jesus and list at least one thing that quality means to you.

Holy —

Harmless —

Undefiled —

Separate from sinners —

Higher than the heavens —

❐ *How does this encourage you to share the good news about Jesus with others?*

3. (7:27-28) *Why did the Levitical high priests have to offer sacrifices first for their own sins?*

❐ *How is Jesus different?*

❐ *What was the sacrifice that Jesus made and why did it only need to be made once?*

❐ *Along with Jesus' qualifications to represent us to God effectively, how do you know that He also is sensitive and compassionate?*

❒ How has this ministry of Jesus as your High Priest affected you?

DIGGING DEEPER

1. Read John 1:29-34. How did John describe Jesus in this brief passage?

❒ How do these descriptions correlate with some of the functions described in Hebrews that Jesus would perform as a high priest?

John's Description   **Hebrews Description**

❒ Why would John describe Jesus (John 1:27) as someone whose shoe latchet he was not worthy to loosen?

❒ What difference has it made to you that Jesus is both the Lamb of God and the Son of God?

2. Read John 10:11-18. Who are the sheep? How is Jesus the Shepherd of the sheep and what does that mean?

❏ *How can Jesus serve as the shepherd when John described Him in John chapter 1 as the lamb?*

❏ *Why was it necessary for Jesus to lay down His life (John 10:15,18)?*

❏ *Why is it important that Jesus said He also would take up His life again (verse 18)?*

❏ *Who are some people with whom you would like to share the good news of Jesus being the Lamb of God?*

❏ *Schedule a time to pray for these people and to ask God to make you sensitive to opportunities for sharing with them. Keep your own record this week to see if you follow through.*

I will pray for	*At this time*	*Did I?*

7

"OH YEAH? WELL MY BLESSINGS ARE THIS BIG!"

The New and the Old
HEBREWS 8:1—9:15

*T*here is no question that the Mosaic Law and all of its requirements and benefits were glorious. God chose Israel, the offspring of Abraham, as His special people (Deuteronomy 7:6-8). He loved them and they returned His love. The law, given at Sinai to Moses was one way God showed his love. David wrote, "O how I love thy law! it is my meditation all the day" (Psalm 119:97).

And all of the worship ceremonies and rituals were wonderful, too. The Tabernacle in the wilderness and, later, the Temple were places where sinful humans could approach a holy and righteous God without being consumed. The sacrificial system and all that accompanied it were established by God as a demonstration of His love and grace.

And yet the system had major limitations. All of the sacrifices and ceremonies were no antidote for the fatal affliction—sin. The best that they could do was to cover the sin of the worshiper until the time that Jesus, the ultimate sacrifice, would die. And when that happened, the entire sacrificial system immediately became irrelevant.

The Old Covenant included a tabernacle and, later, a temple, priests, and sacrifices. But these were given for a limited period of time. And when the final sacrifice of Jesus, the perfect Lamb, was made, there was no more need for repeated sacrifices. Likewise when the eternal high priest took office (according to the order of Melchizedek, not the Levitical order), there was no more need for earthly priests. And rather than having regulations written on tablets of stone, the law of God would be written in the hearts of God's children.

The ultimate expression of this covenant awaits the time when Christ establishes His throne. But today we enjoy the blessings of this new covenant and the ministry of our great high priest.

THE NEW COVENANT IS BETTER THAN THE OLD
(Hebrews 8:1-13)

Jesus, our High Priest, did not come to breathe life into the Old Covenant. Rather, He became the mediator of a totally new covenant.

1. (8:1) *How do we know Jesus' accomplishments were accepted by God?*

❐ *In the Tabernacle (in the wilderness) and the Temple (in Jerusalem) there was no place for the priest to sit down. What is the significance that Jesus, our high priest, sat down in the place of honor?*

❐ *What are some ways that we demonstrate honor to Jesus, our high priest?*

2. (8:2) *Where and what is the "true tabernacle"?*

❐ *Why would Jesus be called a "minister of the sanctuary"?*

3. (8:3) *Since one function of a priest is to offer sacrifices, Jesus also followed this pattern. What sacrifice did Jesus offer?*

4. (8:4-5) *Why would Jesus not have been allowed to be a priest in the earthly sanctuary?*

❐ *What was the purpose of the sanctuary and the sacrifices under the Old Covenant.*

❐ *What truths do these verses teach us about God's expectations and our response?*

❐ *What specific guidelines, given to us by God, do we have today as Christians for approaching Him?*

5. (8:6-8) *The "new promises" will be explained in greater detail in verses 10-13. What three things are better than under the old covenant and why?*

❒ *What was the problem with the old covenant and what was God's solution to these shortcomings?*

Problem   **Solution**

6. (8:9) *This verse refers to the miraculous deliverance of Israel from Egypt. Instead of the expected response, what was the behavior of the Israelites?*

❒ *In what ways are we similar to or different from the Israelites of the Old Testament?*

THE SUPERIORITY OF THE NEW COVENANT (Hebrews 8:10-13)

*G*od's purposes for the old covenant included demonstrating His love for His people and offering them a way to come to Him in spite of their sin. But that covenant was only operative for a limited time, and then it was to be replaced by a new covenant, predicted in Jeremiah 31:31-34.

1. (8:10-12) *Read through these verses and make a list of the characteristics or benefits of the new covenant.*

8:10 1.

2.

8:11   3.

4.

8:12   5.

❏ Which of these conditions do you think exist today?

❏ How do these promises indicate that there will be a future fulfillment of the elements in this new covenant?

❏ Even as the old covenant was with Israel, it appears that the new covenant is also with Israel. Accordingly, the ultimate fulfillment of the new covenant will occur during the Millennium when Christ reigns as Davidic king on earth. And just as non-Jews received blessings under the old covenant, so we in the church today enjoy many of the blessings of the new covenant. Suggest some ways Christians today could appreciate and enjoy these blessings more.

2. (8:13)   This verse probably refers to the continuation of the Old Testament sacrificial system that had not yet terminated when the book of Hebrews was written. Why do you think the Jews were reluctant to abandon the old system?

❐ What blessings do some people today forfeit because they don't understand the promises of the new covenant?

❐ What might be some good things that we should abandon today in order to receive the blessings God wants to give us?

THE EARTHLY AND HEAVENLY PRIESTHOODS (Hebrews 9:1-14)

The earthly tabernacle was built according to exacting specifications and functioned under explicit regulations. And it was of immense benefit to the people. However, the new priesthood is far superior in every way.

1. (9:1-5) List the pieces of the tabernacle furnishings and what each represents.

2. (9:6-7) The "first tabernacle" is the Holy Place (containing the lampstand, the altar of incense and the shewbread) and the "second" the Holy of Holies (containing the ark of the covenant). The high priest entered the Holy of Holies only once a year to offer a sacrifice for the sins of the people. What is the significance of the priest's having to take a blood sacrifice into the Holy of Holies?

3. (9:8) What did the elaborate ceremony and regulations, first in the tabernacle and later in the temple, indicate about access to God under the old covenant?

❏ Read Mark 15:38. What is the significance of the heavy temple curtain being torn from top to bottom when Jesus died?

❏ How does this affect our worship of God today?

4. (9:9-10) What were the limitations of the Old Testament sacrificial system?

5. (9:11-14) As you think about the ways that the new priesthood is better than the old, what does it mean to you personally to experience the blessings of each of these benefits?

A Better Tabernacle (9:11) —

A Better Sacrifice (9:12) —

A Better Cleansing (9:13-14) —

DIGGING DEEPER

1. The Tabernacle and the Temple were earthly places where the presence of God dwelt. In I Corinthians 6:19-20 Paul explains that, for Christians, our bodies are the temple of God's Holy Spirit. How should this influence what we do with our bodies? List similarities that would influence our actions. An example is given.

Temple

Meet with God

My Body

Fellowship with God
because He indwells me

❏ What are some inappropriate ways that people (even sometimes Christians) use their bodies?

❏ What are some very appropriate uses?

❏ What scriptural guidelines can you suggest which would guide your actions.

2. *Read Philippians 3:4-11. In these verses Paul described the many things that had been important to him which he abandoned when he came to Christ. What did Paul choose as a replacement for these things that had meant so much before?*

❑ *What are some things that mean a lot to you but may have little eternal value?*

❑ *What steps should you take to consciously replace things that have little eternal value with something better?*

❖

8

"I DON'T KNOW WHAT IT'S ABOUT. I JUST KNOW IT'S NOT ABOUT CHRISTIANS."

Jesus Christ — the Final Sacrifice
HEBREWS 9:15—10:18

*M*any people struggle with accepting forgiveness for what has happened in the past. Even though Jesus Christ has paid the penalty for their sins and they have been forgiven, they don't *feel* like they have been forgiven. And because they do not *feel* forgiven, many Christians lead lives of frustration burdened with guilt.

Recently Wes counseled with a young man who was very honest and open about what he had done wrong. He had confessed it to God and to the persons he had offended. Intellectually he knew that he had been forgiven, but he claimed that he could not forgive himself. He kept asking what more he could do. And every time

Wes gave the same answer to his question. "There is nothing more you need to do, or can do—Christ did it."

When Jesus Christ died, He paid the penalty for all the sins of all believers—past, present, and future. And this payment was not like the Old Testament sacrifices. They could not forgive sin once and for all. Those sacrifices were made repeatedly and were valid only until the time Christ died and rose again. This is why the author of Hebrews explains, "For it is not possible that the blood of bulls and of goats should take away sins."

It is very easy to confuse *feeling* forgiven with *being* forgiven. And it is easy to confuse *consequences* of sin with *forgiveness* of sin. Even though we have been forgiven, God does not rewrite history to erase the consequences. For example, God forgives the person who commits sexual sin and repents, turning away from it in genuine sorrow. Based on that person's confession, God restores him or her to fellowship. But the pregnancy or the disease, and the damaged relationships resulting from that sin remain facts of history. This is exactly why sin is so personally devastating. It leaves permanent scars.

But this should not make us doubt our forgiveness. Jesus Christ, our perfect High Priest, has made full atonement. He has paid the penalty for our sins.

THE LIMITATIONS OF THE OLD COVENANT (Hebrews 9:15-23)

*T*he words "testament" and "covenant" can be used interchangeably in this section. This concept corresponds to a person's last will and testament today. The testament is a covenant that goes into effect at the death of the one making it.

1. (9:15) *Why did Christ have to die as the mediator of the new covenant (testament)?*

❐ *What promise was fulfilled by what Christ did?*

❏ What is the promise of eternal inheritance?

❏ Is this inheritance yours? How do you know?

2. (9:16-17) What is the relationship between the promises of the new covenant and the death of Jesus Christ?

3. (9:18-22) These verses refer to Moses' ratification of the old covenant (Exodus 24:3-8) and the institution of the sacrificial system. How do the detailed requirements of the old covenant help us understand the seriousness of sin?

4. (9:23) The "patterns" (literally, "the copies"—the tabernacle, including the sacrificial system) could be purified by animal sacrifices, but the reality behind the tabernacle could not be. What "better sacrifice" could purify heavenly things?

THE ADVANTAGES OF THE NEW COVENANT
Hebrews 9:24-28

*T*he new sanctuary and the sacrifice are infinitely better than the old. The old was earthly and involved repeated sacrifices. The new is heavenly and requires only the sacrifice of Jesus Christ, the Son of God Himself.

1. (9:24) What is the relationship between the old holy places and the new?

❏ What are some of the things that you would like Jesus to do for you as He stands continually before God?

2. (9:25-26) Why did the Old Testament priests have to offer sacrifices repeatedly while Jesus only had to die once for all our sins?

3. (9:27) After death, how will the eternal position of believers be different from the position of unbelievers?

❏ Why would people want to believe they get a second chance after death to change their eternal destiny or believe that they come back in reincarnation? How does this verse answer those ideas?

4. (9:28) When Jesus appears the second time without sin, who will be watching for Him?

❏ Do you feel that your salvation makes a significant difference in your daily life? Why or why not? How does it affect your life?

JESUS CHRIST, THE PERFECT SACRIFICE
(Hebrews 10:1-18)

*T*he Mosaic Law and the Old Testament sacrificial system were established for a specific purpose and for a limited period of time. Part of that purpose was to point people to Christ. And now that He has come, we no longer need the old system.

1. (10:1-3) *What are some of the reasons that we can say with complete assurance that the Old Testament sacrifices could not ultimately solve the sin problem?*

2. (10:4-10) *What are some contrasts between the Old Testament sacrifices and the sacrifice of Jesus? (You may want to look at Exodus 30:1-10 and Leviticus 7:1-10.)*

    OT Sacrifices   **Jesus' Sacrifice**

3. (10:11-14) *What are some contrasts between the priest who made the offerings in the Old Testament and Jesus Christ, our perfect high priest? (You may want to look at Exodus 29 and Leviticus 8.)*

    OT Priest   **Jesus Our High Priest**

❐ *Why was a blood sacrifice necessary as an atonement for sin?*

❒ List some ways that Christians in a local church can demonstrate, as a group, their deep appreciation for and recognition of Christ's sacrifice for them.

4. (10:15-18) How have the "laws of God" been written in our hearts and minds?

❒ In what sense do we look to the future for the complete fulfillment of this condition?

❒ Look at God's promise to you in verses 17-18. What does it mean to you to know that God, with the witness of His Holy Spirit, has chosen to forget your sins?

DIGGING DEEPER

1. It is very important that we act on the basis of what we know to be true and not necessarily on how we feel. Why do you think that sometimes we may not feel forgiven?

❒ What suggestions can you make to a person who has sinned, has confessed that sin, and knows that he or she is forgiven, yet does not "feel forgiven"?

2. *Jesus paid the penalty for all of our sins when He died, and He pleads our case with the Father (I John 2:1-2). Yet it is important to confess specific acts of sin that we commit after accepting Christ. This is not to keep us saved (Jesus does that) but to maintain our fellowship with Christ. Read I John 1:9-10. Why might Christians be reluctant to confess—and stop doing—sin? What does confession involve?*

☐ *Is it important to you to maintain an open, constant fellowship with Jesus? How would sin keep you from that?*

☐ *Do you need to experience the cleansing ministry of Christ? Are there sins you need to confess and turn away from? Identify areas of your greatest struggles and ask God for grace and strength to keep your life in these areas clean before the Lord.*

3. *Hebrews 9:28 and I John 3:1-3 speak of Christ's future return to earth and the Father's love. Think of specific areas of your life. How should these truths and the certainty of seeing Christ motivate you and affect your thoughts and actions?*

9

"IS IT STILL A GOOD WORK IF IT'S VEGETABLES?"

Encouragement to Christian Living
HEBREWS 10:19-39

*T*here are few feelings more difficult to manage than the feeling that we are all alone. Early in life most children need reassurance that there is someone near them. Some children don't want to go off to their bedrooms at night because they will be alone. It is normal for children as they are growing up to go through a period of time when they don't want to be left with a babysitter.

But even as we grow older, we continue to have needs that can only be met through relationships. No matter how confident and secure we may become, we will never outgrow the need for support and encouragement. These can only come from others, through relationships with people we trust—those who will be there when we need them.

The prophet Elijah won an incredible victory over the prophets of Baal. But in spite of the wonderful demonstration of God's power that confirmed Elijah's authority, he sank into depression. It seemed to Elijah that all of the other spiritual leaders had defected and that only he had remained true to God. He felt that everyone had abandoned him and that he was alone (I Kings 18:1—19:14).

One of the bleakest moments in the life of Christ came when His closest friends were not available in His time of need. We read of Christ's sorrowful question when He asked His three close friends—Peter, James, and John— why they could not pray with Him for even one hour when He needed them (Matthew 26:40).

The author of Hebrews admonishes us in this fourth warning that we must not treat sin casually. All of us need the encouragement that comes from Christ and from other believers to follow through on our commitment to serve and to obey the Lord.

ENCOURAGEMENT TO RIGHTEOUS LIVING (Hebrews 10:19-25)

We have the wonderful privilege of full access to the throne of God at any moment. And we can come confidently, knowing that Jesus Christ has fully opened the way for us through His death.

1. (10:19-20) *How can you enter "the holiest"? (In the Old Testament the Holy of Holies was the place where the priest met with God.)*

❏ *How does this further explain the tearing of the veil in the temple (Matthew 27:51)? What does it mean?*

❐ *What are some of the benefits you have by being able to approach God directly today?*

❐ *What should you guard against in coming to God so easily?*

2. (10:21-22) *What is the house of God?*

❐ *How do you draw near to God? Is there anything that keeps you from living close to Him?*

❐ *What changes might you need to make in the way that you communicate with God?*

3. (10:23) *Even though we are not always faithful, what is the basis on which we can be confident of our relationship with Christ?*

❐ *What specific demonstrations of Christ's faithfulness encourage consistency in your Christian walk?*

4. (10:24) *How can believers encourage others to express love and good works?*

❐ Who has encouraged you in your Christian walk, and how did they do it?

❐ Who may be looking to you for encouragement in their spiritual lives?

5. (10:25)   What day is approaching?

❐ What is the benefit of believers gathering together?

BEWARE A CASUAL ATTITUDE TOWARD SIN (Hebrews 10:26-31)

*J*esus died for our sins, and we will not have to pay for them. But we must be all the more careful not to approach sin casually. Justification by Christ's death is no excuse for a careless attitude toward sin.

1. (10:26)   *This particular warning is against a cavalier attitude toward sin. Just because we have been forgiven doesn't mean that we can now sin whenever we want. What are some of the ways that we receive knowledge of what is sin?*

❐ Do you ever sin willfully? Why? What keeps you from sinning more often?

2. (10:27)   *We know that Christ has paid the penalty for our sins which means that we will not suffer eternal judgment for*

them. But we do experience God's discipline. What are some ways that God disciplines us?

❏ Who would be an adversary and experience God's judgment and discipline?

3. (10:28-29) What was the Old Testament standard for judgment?

❏ Why does God's standard today make us deserving of greater punishment?

❏ How can we spite the Spirit of grace?

❏ Why is a believer's sin such an offense to God?

❏ Based on these verses, describe how God views the sin that we might consider to be relatively unimportant.

4. (10:30-31) How do we know that this warning is addressed to Christians?

❏ Why is it "fearful" to be judged by God? Are you afraid of the penalty or discipline your sin deserves?

❏ *What warning can you appropriately give to a Christian who seems indifferent to his or her sinful actions?*

ENCOURAGEMENT TO FAITHFULNESS AND ENDURANCE (Hebrews 10:32-39)

What a revitalizing truth to know that we are not alone as we try to live a Christ-like life! Not only do we have the encouragement of Christ, but we also draw strength from each other. And this encouragement spurs us on to grow and to thrive in the midst of difficulty.

1. (10:32-34) *How could remembering earlier afflictions help you today?*

❏ *Why would salvation (illumination) bring about affliction or trouble?*

❏ *Even if our life situations never get any better, what do we have to look forward to ultimately?*

❏ *In what instances can you remember receiving comfort from knowing that this life is not "the end?"*

2. (10:35-37) *How is the encouragement of these verses a good balance to the earlier warning in verses 26-31?*

❏ *Why is patience important in the Christian life?*

❏ *What is the importance of patience in doing the will of God? How can you do the will of God?*

❏ *What are some areas where you might find it difficult to wait patiently for God to work?*

❏ *What is the ultimate promise for which all believers should be waiting?*

3. (10:38-39) *How could the writer of Hebrews be sure that he and his readers were not those who would "draw back unto perdition"?*

❏ *In practical terms, how do you live by faith?*

❏ *What evidences in your life demonstrate that you have faith and did not "draw back?"*

DIGGING DEEPER

1. *How would you answer someone who claims that it's really not vital to fellowship and study the Bible with other Christians?*

❐ *Based on what you have studied in this epistle, evaluate and reply to the comment, "I feel so much closer to God when I am in the out-of-doors. I don't feel that I need to get dressed up and sit in a building on Sunday morning with a bunch of other people. I would much rather worship God alone, quietly and meditatively." What attitudes does such a statement really reflect?*

2. *When do you regularly meet with other believers?*

❐ *Why do you participate in these gatherings (i.e. Bible study, prayer, etc.)?*

❐ *What things sometimes keep you from participating in these times with other Christians?*

3. *The seriousness of habitual sin for believers today is not something to be taken casually. How do you recognize and deal with sin in your life?*

❐ *Are there some things in your life now that need to be confessed and forsaken? Are you willing to confess them? Why or why not? What keeps you from turning away from those sins and doing what God wants?*

❐ *Take some time to evaluate your life and to confess any thoughts, deeds, or attitudes that might need to be dealt with.*

❖

10

Examples of the Faith Life
HEBREWS 11:1-40

*M*ost of us can identify specific people who have influenced us greatly. That person may be a parent or an older brother or sister. Many people also recall teachers who had a profound influence in their lives.

When Wes was a student in elementary school he had one unlikely hero. It wasn't a teacher. Wes's hero was the school janitor who had his own room with many fascinating tools. And it was a great day whenever Wes was asked to run an errand that took him to the janitor's room!

We may be completely unaware of how much certain individuals have influenced us. Many of us hear ourselves using an expression that we recall hearing our parents say. And we are startled to recognize how we have absorbed (without even realizing it) certain patterns of response in a given situation. Unfortunately, it is not only the positives that we pick up from others; we also can mimic negative behaviors.

The author of Hebrews knew how important good models are. So when he moves into a discussion of what it means to live the faith life, he does more than just tell us how to live by faith. Rather, he gives us example after example of those who have gone before us. None of these people were perfect and God doesn't hesitate to show how they failed. Yet these are Old Testament (and some New Testament) believers who lived by faith and who serve as good models for us today.

But it is important to remember that in most cases these believers died without ever seeing the cornerstone of their faith with their physical eyes. The nature of faith is that even though we cannot physically observe the fulfillment of a promise, we accept it as already having been fulfilled. In this way, each person recorded in Hebrews 11 demonstrated faith. Each one saw God's promises as reality and acted on that reality.

INTRODUCTION TO FAITH
(Hebrews 11:1-3)

*B*efore plunging into a series of examples of faith in action, the author of Hebrews gives a brief definition of what faith is.

1. (11:1) *The definition of faith given here is basic, without illustrations. These will come later. "Substance" refers to "assurance" and "evidence" is "proof." Try to think of some illustrations of things today that you hope for by faith and of which you can be assured.*

❒ *What things do you accept as proof even though you cannot see them?*

2. (11:2) *How does the presence of faith in a person's life enable us to give a good report about them to others?*

❏ *What are some evidences of faith in your life that you think others might cite as positive references to your character?*

3. (11:3) *How was the "word of God" instrumental in framing the world (cf. Genesis 1:3,6,9,11,14,20,24; John 1:1-3; Colossians 1:15-17)?*

❏ *How does our present understanding of molecular structure enhance the statement that the "things which are seen were not made of things which do appear?"*

❏ *How could this increase our faith in the reality of God's promises?*

THE FAITH THAT PLEASES GOD
(Hebrews 11:4-16)

Old Testament saints were accepted by God for their faith, not for what they did. However, their actions demonstrated their faith.

1. *Some believers given as faith examples are listed below; read the Old Testament references where their actions are* recorded. For each character, identify the primary action that demonstrated faith and write it in the "HERO OF FAITH" column. Then, describe how you can demonstrate similar faith today.

	HERO OF FAITH	MY FAITH TODAY
(11:4) Abel Genesis 4:3-5		
(11:5) Enoch Genesis 5:22-24		
(11:7) Noah Genesis 6:13-22		
(11:8-10,12) Abraham Genesis 12:1-4, 15:5-6, 23:4		
(11:11) Sarah Genesis 17:15-19, 21:1-7		

2. **(11:6)** What are the components of faith in this verse?

❏ Why are these essential elements of faith?

❏ *What are some specific actions in your life that demonstrate these elements of faith?*

3. (11:13) *What separated these heroes of faith from most of their contemporaries?*

❏ *How should "strangers and pilgrims" behave in a place where they dwell only temporarily?*

❏ *In what ways do many Christians in our churches today act more like settlers than like strangers or pilgrims?*

❏ *Which description would better characterize you personally, and why would you conclude this?*

4. (11:14-16) *What city were these Old Testament believers seeking?*

❏ *What are some of the characteristics of that city?*

❏ *How does this truth complement what Jesus said in John 14:1-6?*

❏ *What excites you when you think about the city where we will dwell for all eternity?*

VARIOUS DEMONSTRATIONS OF FAITH
(Hebrews 11:17-40)

*I*t is interesting to see who the writer of Hebrews, under the inspiration of the Holy Spirit, selected as examples of godly faith, highlighting many who are well-known to us and some whose identification is more obscure.

1. (11:17-19) *How did Abraham demonstrate his faith (cf. Genesis 22:1-18)?*

❏ *What did he expect God to do for him and for Isaac (cf. Genesis 15:5-6)?*

❏ *In what ways might you be called to give up a loved one to God?*

2. (11:20-22) *What are some ways we might treat our children that demonstrate our faith in God?*

3. (11:23) *How did Moses' parents demonstrate their faith (cf. Exodus 1—2)?*

4. (11:24-26) *Moses was raised in the palace, as Pharaoh's grandson. How do you think he learned to have such faith in God and know the treasures of God's rewards?*

❏ *What are some difficult decisions that Moses had to make because he was a man of faith?*

❏ *Under what circumstances might you need to make some similar decisions?*

5. (11:27-31) Even though God worked miracles for those who followed Him, most of the time they had to act and later God confirmed that they had made the right decisions. How is this true in the experiences of...

Moses   **Joshua**   **Rahab**

❏ *When have you needed to act on faith and then had God later confirm that you had done the right thing?*

❏ *Think of a decision that you must make at the present time that requires faith in God.*

❏ *How will you know God's will?*

❏ *How do you expect God to confirm this action? When do you expect confirmation—now or later?*

6. (11:32-37) In some parts of the world today Christians still experience torture and persecutions similar to what is recorded here. Identify some of those countries and how Christians might be suffering.

❑ We face different persecution in this country. What are some things that we might be called to endure in faith?

❑ How could you and Christians you know support believers who are experiencing persecution?

7. (11:38)   What does it mean that the world was not worthy of these?

8. (11:39-40)   Why would these earlier Christians not be perfect (complete) without us?

DIGGING DEEPER

1. Look up the other Old Testament believers whom God gave us as examples of faith. Identify the primary action, why it demonstrates faith, and then describe how you can demonstrate similar faith today.

	Why This Hero/Action Demonstrates Faith	**My Faith**
(11:30) Joshua (Joshua 6)		
(11:31) Rahab (Joshua 2,6:22-23)		
(11:32) Gideon (Judges 7)		

	Why This **Hero/Action** **Demonstrates Faith**	**My Faith**
(11:32) Barak *(Judges 4)*		
(11:32) Samson *(Judges 15)*		
(11:32) Jephthah *(Judges 11-12)*		

2. *List some people living today whom you would describe as "people of faith" and why. Include any impact they have had in your life.*

Person/Action	**Why This** **Demonstrates Faith**

3. *When have you found it difficult to believe God? Why?*

❐ *Describe a time when God has chosen to reward your faith by giving you some evidence of the fact that He is at work in your life.*

❐ *Spend time in prayer explaining to God what you struggle with believing and ask Him to strengthen your weak faith.*

95

11

"IT'S SIMPLE. YOU JUST PRAY FOR THE COURAGE TO OVERCOME YOUR PROBLEMS. JESUS KNOWS WHICH ONES."

Becoming All God Wants Us to Be
HEBREWS 12:1-29

As we observed our own children growing up, we learned a lot about human nature. And as we observed other parents relating to their children, those lessons have been reinforced.

For example, we learned that children need and desire structure and discipline in life, but they often tend to grumble and complain when guidelines are enforced.

When our boys were young, sometimes they would ask for permission to do something that we felt was unwise. And when we denied them permission, sometimes they would argue and complain. Usually they asked the question children have asked their parents for generations, "But why?" Sometimes we were able to give a good reason. But other times the explanation was something that they probably couldn't understand.

At times like that, occasionally we resorted to a strategy of giving a ridiculous answer to get our message across. "Because we dislike you very much and are doing everything that we can to make you the most miserable creatures on the face of this earth." Inevitably this response would evoke some resigned acceptance of the decision and often even a chuckle or two.

Our point was that we were not being arbitrary or insensitive, but that we really loved our sons very much. And even if they did not always understand our reasoning, we did have a sensible, logical basis for the decisions that we made. Our intent was to help them grow and become all that they could be—all that God wanted them to be.

God disciplines us in a similar way, but with infinitely greater love and goals for His children. Because of this, we can rejoice that He is in the process of helping us grow toward maturity. He longs for us to be mature, consistent followers of Christ.

DISCIPLINE IN THE CHRISTIAN LIFE (Hebrews 12:1-17)

*I*t is not the easy times but the difficult ones that build strength and maturity in our lives. However, it is important to know that we do not struggle through the difficult times alone. Our Lord and Savior Jesus Christ encourages and ministers to us.

1. **(12:1)** *This "cloud of witnesses" is often described as fans watching from the grandstand. But they are witnesses who give testimony to the fact that living by faith is the best way. From your study of chapter 11, summarize how the persons described in that chapter bear witness to the validity of the faith life.*

❐ *Runners don't wear work boots and overcoats when they race. They try to eliminate all excess weight. How are our* sins like weights that would hinder us from running in the race of life competitively?

❐ Which kinds of sin "easily beset" you?

2. (12:2) *How is Jesus the author and finisher of our faith?*

author —

finisher —

3. (12:3-4) *No matter what we endure, it is less than what Jesus experienced. List some of the events of Jesus' life that the author of Hebrews is probably referring to here.*

4. (12:5-8) *Discipline is more than punishment. It also includes guidance, character-shaping, and strength-building. What are two ways that we can respond to discipline?*

❐ How is discipline an ingredient of love?

❐ Has God ever disciplined you? Why? What did you learn from it or how did you grow through His discipline?

❐ What was the long term benefit?

❏ *How do you know or recognize when God is disciplining you?*

❏ *How does viewing God as a loving father give us a unique perspective on difficult times we might endure?*

6. (12:9) *What is the comparison suggested between our earthly fathers who disciplined us and our heavenly Father?*

❏ *What challenges does this verse present to fathers of children today? And what challenge to us as children of God?*

7. (12:10-11) *What differences and similarities are there between our earthly parents' discipline and our heavenly Father's discipline?*

Differences   Similarities

❏ *How do we generally respond in the midst of being disciplined?*

❏ *And how do we respond when we look back on the experience later?*

8. (12:12-14) *What attitudes should we have during a period of discipline?*

❏ How does the fact of knowing that God is disciplining you for your good help you to thrive victoriously in the midst of the difficulties?

❏ What kinds of difficulties in your life can you pause and thank God for right now, knowing that He is producing holiness (godly character) through those experiences?

9. (12:15-17) If we choose not to grow through discipline, we may instead become bitter. How does bitterness affect a Christian? What are some consequences of bitterness in a believer's life?

❏ Look carefully at your life. Are there any "roots" of bitterness trying to spring up in your life? Anger against a former employer or present employer, against a family member, against a friend? Why do you feel bitterness toward them?

❏ You may feel justified in your bitterness (and anger) because of what someone did to you, but how does God view your attitude?

❏ Take some time to confess any bitterness that you identify, and ask God to help you grow in holiness through the circumstances rather than allow the bitterness to continue in your life.

WARNING AGAINST IGNORING JESUS
(Hebrews 12:18-29)

*I*f ignoring God's commands in the Old Testament was punished so severely, how much more careful we should be about paying attention to what Jesus Christ has said!

1. (12:18-21) *These historical events are recorded in Exodus 19 which describes how God gave Moses the law on Mount Sinai. How did God demonstrate the seriousness of what He was doing and stress that the people needed to give careful attention?*

❏ *Do you feel that people today give greater or less reverence to God's Word? Why?*

2. (12:22-23) *Instead of encountering God on Mount Sinai, where do we encounter Him?*

❏ *Who else comes before God and how does their inclusion impact us?*

3. (12:24) *What role does Jesus have in this relationship that we have with God today?*

❏ *What is meant by the reference to Abel's blood?*

4. (12:25-26) *What parallel does the author of Hebrews make between how the Israelites listened at the giving of the law and how we should listen to Jesus today?*

❏ *What are some of the teachings of Jesus that you think Christians today may neglect?*

❏ *How can you insure that you are alert to Jesus' teachings and are following in obedience?*

5. (12:26-29) *What are some non-permanent things that can (and will) be removed?*

❏ *And what are some things that will never be shaken or removed?*

❏ *In a short paragraph, describe how grace, service, reverence, and godly fear (verse 28) should fit together in a practical way in a Christian's life today.*

DIGGING DEEPER

1. *Read through Mark 14:32—15:41 noting the animosity, agony, and suffering that Jesus endured. Jesus submitted Himself to this treatment for us so that we could be made righteous. How should we respond?*

❐ What are some of the difficulties that you encounter in life specifically because you are a Christian?

❐ What other difficulties do you struggle with simply because they are part of life in a fallen world?

❐ Spend some time in prayer telling God about those concerns. Ask Christ specifically to encourage and strengthen you, knowing that He endured far more for us than we could ever imagine facing in our daily lives.

2. Hebrews 12:22-25 reminds us of our spiritual "roots" in Heaven. Read II Peter 3:9-14 and summarize Peter's description of these future events.

❐ What warning is given to unbelievers?

❐ How should knowing these prophecies influence Christians every day?

❖

12

"MOTHER AND I HAVE A GREAT RELATION-
SHIP — EXCEPT WHEN SHE TRIES TO
FEED ME SPINACH."

Loving and Obeying God
HEBREWS 13

*T*here are few things more dreadful to contemplate than religious fervor built on counterfeit Christianity. Over the centuries, there have been many wars waged in the name of Christianity. But most of the participants were expressing blind zeal, not biblical Christianity.

One of the ways we see such counterfeit Christianity today is in cultic organizations that work to control behavior rather than to nurture a relationship with Jesus Christ. Like any counterfeit, such movements contain elements that appear to be true, but a vital element is always missing. Two errors are prevalent in all such counterfeits: 1) a distortion of (or addition to) the Word of God, and 2) a denial of the clear message of salvation by grace through faith in Jesus Christ alone.

It may be a Jim Jones in Guyana or David Koresh in Waco. Or it can be a local group, without national visibility, that controls its members by demanding ritualistic and legalistic observance of cultic practices. Such groups tend to share a common perversion. They teach a distortion of the message of grace and observe rituals that focus on external behavior and blind obedience to autocratic leaders. Inevitably, such autocratic control leads to a violation of biblical principles.

This phenomenon is not new. In New Testament times false teachers were already distorting the message of grace, and some leaders were trying to control the behavior of their followers through ritualistic demands. In this final chapter of Hebrews, God gives us guidelines for the day-to-day practical application of Christianity. We are challenged to relate to one another properly, relate to our leaders appropriately, and nurture practices that reflect a genuine relationship with Jesus Christ.

OUR SERVICE TO FELLOW CHRISTIANS (Hebrews 13:1-6)

*T*his final chapter begins with instructions about interpersonal relationships concerning hospitality, morality, and our attitudes toward the material possessions of others.

1. **(13:1-2)** *Although many Christians profess to love and serve God with sincerity, why do some of them treat other people, especially other Christians, poorly?*

❒ *How is hospitality one way in which we can demonstrate our love for God and for others?*

❒ *Many have suggested that people today are less*

hospitable than former generations. Do you think that this is true? Why or why not?

2. (13:3) *How could Christians today remember "them that are in bonds?"*

❐ *List some Christians you are aware of who are suffering adversity. In what tangible ways could you or fellow Christians assist them?*

    Persons   ***Ways to Help***

3. (13:4) *Our society often uses the word "love" to describe illicit sexual relationships. In what sense is adultery exactly the opposite of love?*

❐ *Why will God judge those who engage in illicit sexual relationships (whoremongers) and those who are unfaithful to their spouses (adulterers)?*

❐ *What is God's view of sexual relationships within the context of marriage?*

4. (13:5-6) *The Greek word for "conversation" includes the way we talk as well as our entire manner of living—our* *attitudes, behavior, and values. How is covetousness expressed among people today?*

❏ *How do the media glorify and actually promote covetous values and attitudes?*

❏ *What makes you discontent with what you have? How can you resist the pressures to focus on material things rather than being satisfied with God and His current provisions in your life?*

❏ *In what ways are we freed from bondage to material possessions by a proper attitude toward God?*

OUR SERVICE TO GOD
(Hebrews 13:7-19)

*B*elievers have certain obligations in their worship and obedience to God, and we also have many blessings secured for us by Christ's sacrifice. Our response to God is a sacrifice of praise!

1. **(13:7)** *Why is it important to follow godly spiritual leaders?*

2. **(13:8-9)** *How does the consistent, unchanging nature of Jesus relate to consistency in our doctrine?*

❏ What are some external, ritualistic regulations that churchgoers have tried to substitute for a true heart relationship with Jesus Christ?

❏ What unchanging doctrines do people try to change to accommodate society or personal desires?

3. (13:10-12) The picture presented in these verses contrasts the temporary regulations of the Mosaic system with the new system following the sacrifice of Christ. What are some parallels of the two systems seen in these verses and what elements are different?

❏ Jesus died "without the gate." Does this have any implications for His followers today?

4. (13:13-14) How can you "go forth" for Jesus?

❏ What are some situations when you might be called upon to "bear His reproach"?

❏ How does the fact that this life is not our final goal help us to focus on what's important and deal with difficulties that we might encounter?

5. (13:15-16) *God still wants sacrifices today. But what kind of sacrifices does He expect from us?*

❏ *In what ways can you give these sacrifices? (Note that the Greek word for "communicate" is koinonea, meaning "fellowship" or "sharing.")*

6. (13:17) *This verse has been distorted and abused by many who want to exert illegitimate control over their followers. It is not a blanket endorsement of all leaders, nor is it a mandate to do whatever you are told, whether right or wrong. Why, when, and how should we obey spiritual leaders?*

❏ *What clear responsibilities and expectations for church leaders are stated?*

❏ *How can we who are followers determine whether our leaders serve joyfully or with great burden?*

7. (13:18-19) *What are the obligations of all Christians?*

CLOSING COMMENTS AND BENEDICTION
(Hebrews 13:20-25)

*I*n these few closing words the author speaks encouragement and summarizes his desire for the Hebrew Christians. He longs for them to reach full maturity in Christ.

1. (13:20-21) *"Make you perfect" refers to becoming mature, not flawless. What is the purpose for our maturity?*

❐ *Describe something in your life that has changed as you have become increasingly mature spiritually.*

2. (13:22-23) *How do these final verses demonstrate the author's sensitivity and concern for fellow believers?*

❐ *How have you seen similar concern expressed by your spiritual leaders?*

3. (13:24-25) *What are some of the ways that God has bestowed His grace upon you?*

❐ *Take a few minutes to thank God for the abundant blessings that He has showered upon you as manifestations of grace.*

DIGGING DEEPER

1. *The predominant emphasis of the book of Hebrews has been the ministry of Jesus Christ. Not only is He our eternal High Priest (the one who represents us to God), but He is also our sacrifice. In this role, He alone is our mediator, the one who provides access to God. This is why we pray in His name. As our High Priest, He also prays for us. Read John 17, Jesus' intercessory prayer for His disciples. What were some of the deep concerns that Jesus expressed in these verses?*

❐ *What would you like to ask Jesus to intercede with God for you?*

2. *Review some of the major truths you have learned from the book of Hebrews. Which of these stand out in your mind as concepts that were new to you or were particularly helpful to you in your personal life and growth?*

❐ *What are some areas in your life where you still need to experience spiritual victory?*

❐ *Select a verse or passage from Hebrews to memorize as a reminder of your spiritual blessings and your commitment to obeying and serving God.*